CHRISTINE BOWLER **Between the Broken Glass the People Play** is both the story of the end of an affair and an affirmation of life. Different people are reflected, come alive in the splinters, pieces of glass.

Christine Bowler was born in London in 1945. She started work as a newspaper reporter writing on the pop scene. She is living in Wales and working on a novel **And There Are Moments that Shock Me.**

LYMAN ANDREWS **'The Death of Mayakovsky' and other Poems** is written with great simplicity and power. Lyman Andrews poetry has appeared in two collections **Ash Flowers,** 1958 and **Fugitive Visions** 1962 and in many magazines including **Evergreen Review** and **Transatlantic Review.**

He was born in 1938 in Denver, Colorado and was educated in Boston, London and Berkeley. He has been living in England since 1963 and is a lecturer in American Studies at the University of Leicester. He is Poetry critic of the Sunday Times.

F. W. WILLETTS **Cunard in the Desert** is a concrete story which through the words and through the shape of the print shows a man trying to conquer loneliness and silence.

F. W. Willetts writes radio plays for the B.B.C. His plays have been broadcast in Germany, Sweden, Italy and the United States and televised in Yugoslavia and Czechoslovakia. In 1967 a collection of his poems **Some Notes From Cunard** was published by the Golden Head Press

RED DUST 1

New Writing

Christine Bowler

BETWEEN THE BROKEN GLASS THE PEOPLE PLAY

Lyman Andrews

THE DEATH OF MAYAKOVSKY

F. W. Willetts

CUNARD IN THE DESERT

RED DUST · NEW YORK

Originally published as New Writers VIII
by Calder and Boyars Ltd, 1968

Published in the United States of America
by Red Dust Inc. 1970

L.C.C. no 78 127954

SBN 87376 017 4 Paper edition
SBN 87376 016 6 Cloth edition

PRINTED IN GREAT BRITAIN BY
NORTHUMBERLAND PRESS LIMITED
GATESHEAD

CONTENTS

Christine Bowler

BETWEEN THE BROKEN GLASS THE PEOPLE PLAY

UNABLE TO BELIEVE IN YOU AS YOU STAND THERE; GASPING SILENTLY AS YOU MOVE ACROSS MY PATH. THERE IS A SHIMMERING ON THIS AFTERNOON; AND THE SKY IS VERY HIGH OVER THE WOODS BURNISHED WITH SUMMER.

PERHAPS IF I HAD SEEN THE RESURRECTION IT WOULD HAVE BEEN LIKE THIS? WE STAND FRONT TO FRONT, A FEW FEET APART, WITH ONLY THE GRASS BETWEEN US. THE GRASS IS GROWING GREENER WITH OUR MOMENTS. AND WE RUN FORWARD TO MEET OURSELVES FOR SHELTER ON THIS ETERNAL AFTERNOON.

YOU SAY HOW TOLERANT I AM BECAUSE I DO NOT MIND THE MUD. AND WE RACE, AND YOU PULL ME DOWN ON SOME DRY GRASS, AND WE CLAMBER UP FOR IT IS FULL OF HIDDEN WATER. THE GRASS IS CRYING TEARS. IT MUST KNOW OF THE FUTURE.

TOGETHER WE SWIM ON THE WIND AS THE KITES FLY WITH US, BLIND TO NOTHING: GOING TO LOOK AT A BIG, DEAD MUSEUM OF A HOUSE; PEERING THROUGH THE WINDOWS AT THE ORNAMENTAL FURNITURE. WE HAVE TEA INSTEAD. AND THEN RETURNING TO THE DUSTY ROOM EAT CORN FLOATING IN BUTTER; AND FLOW AGAIN INTO THE OTHER, WHILE THE AFTERNOON DYING LIVES ON THOUGH LONG DEAD.

I REMEMBER SO MUCH AND SO LITTLE. TIME HAS STOLEN WHAT HAPPENED. WE HAVE KILLED EACH OTHER AND STILL GO ON LIVING. WHILE BETWEEN US THE PEOPLE PLAY . . .

BUT I RECALL A LOST SUMMER DAY WHEN WE WERE LIKE CHILDREN IN A NURSERY. IT WAS VERY HOT AND THE HEAT SIMMERED IN THROUGH A SKYLIGHT. WE WORE NO DISGUISE, AND THE SUN JOINED OUR GAMES OF INNOCENCE AND DELIGHT. WE WANDERED IN THE STREETS, MY HAIR LONG OVER MY SHOULDERS, AND YOU BESIDE ME BRINGING LIFE ALIVE. WE WERE HAPPY.

A DAY BY THE RIVER WHEN WE CAUGHT SILVER.

A MOON UPON A FROZEN NIGHT AND YOU POINTED OUT THE BRIGHTEST STAR IN THE SKY, YOU WERE GOING TO WRITE A BOOK ABOUT IT. REMEMBER?

Remember . . .

WHY DID YOU HAVE TO SMASH ALL THIS? WHY DID YOU BREAK ALL THIS? YOU SHATTERED A WORLD INSIDE MY HEAD AND BANGED ME UP AGAINST THE WALL UNTIL I SAW RAINBOWS AND FELT ONLY FEAR.

YOU HIT ME AS IF I WAS SUCH AN ENEMY. YOU HATED ME FOR GRADUALLY YOU KNEW YOU WERE MY MURDERER, AND YOUR OWN. AND YOU FELL AGAINST ME AND CRIED SUCH TERRIBLE HOT TEARS. I CRIED TOO, FROM SHOCK. OUR TEARS WERE DIFFERENT.

AND YOU HIT THE WALL WITH YOUR FIST LIKE RUBBER. AND YOU PICKED UP THE GLASS OVER THE FIRE WITH 'I LOVE YOU' SMEARED OVER IT. I WROTE IT ONE MORNING. YOU

COULD NOT FORGET. YOU THREW THE MIRROR THROUGH THE WINDOW. AND I RAN INTO THE BATHROOM. AND THEN THERE WAS A LOT OF NOISE. SO MUCH NOISE.

HEAVEN AND EARTH WAS BEING BROKEN. ALL THE WINDOWS. DREAMS.

THERE WAS A GIRL IN THE BATHROOM WASHING. WE CLUNG TOGETHER IN THE DARKNESS.

AND WHEN YOU HAD FINISHED YOUR SMASHING YOU CALLED FOR ME AND I RAN WITH YOU. I WAS FRIGHTENED ON THAT TRAIN. AND YOU, YOU WERE MARVELLING AT THE LIGHTS ON THE RIVER, AS IT PULLED OUT TAKING US NOWHERE.

NOW YOU HAVE SMASHED EVERYTHING—WHILE BETWEEN THE BROKEN GLASS THE PEOPLE PLAY . . .

First there is a man, a deaf man. A middle-aged man who hasn't heard a single noise since he was eighteen and a bomb shattered his ears. The bomb just dropped.

He lives in his head with the sounds he can still hear from over twenty years, and listens with his eyes to silent lips that speak with movements. Sometimes it is difficult to understand what he is saying for he speaks very softly for fear of shouting. But you smile and pretend you hear everything, and reply, although you know he is often unable to understand your lips because you mumble.

The warmth of a smile will not elude him. And he knows what it is when he sees a man with one leg putting shillings in a one-armed bandit. He spends a lot of time in pubs but won't forget. He asked if they still ring bells at closing time.

The only music he hears is the hit songs of the war years and the melodies of childhood. But he sings nursery rhymes to his new baby and says she enjoys it.

Yesterday he wrote a line that said: 'God's in his heaven—God's all right.'

Now he is distressed and depressed because suddenly sitting opposite him is a soulless young man with a black, bushy beard. Not only is he unable to understand his soullessness but his lips. His lips are covered with hair and no one else noticed.

He is very efficient, this black-bearded man. He must believe it compensates for his lack of awareness. He plasters the walls with charts and makes the office look like a betting shop with large sheets of cardboard with dates on in big, black letters. Knowing how to spell every word in the English language perfectly and not having the slightest notion of what to do with it, he would be frightened to define the meaning of the word LOVE.

SISTER MARY STEPHEN AT SCHOOL HEARD PERFECTLY. She heard every whisper. She enjoyed the silence of the chapel broken only by the rustle of the black robes; and squeaky shoes; and the rattle of rosaries.

She spoke in a crisp voice as starchy as the bandeau that hides her forehead forever. Twisting and playing with the wedding ring on her left hand. Married to God. Her hands square and stubby touch nothing soft.

Always in a hurry. Always head before feet and veil flowing behind in a hymn of its own. She wore tortoiseshell glasses, and was very strict and well-scrubbed of the world. The motto of the order—TRUTH.

There was Sister Ambrose, face scarred with tiny, crisscross lines. Ancient. She had glasses with the tops cut off like crescent moons, and peered over them. She said it was GOOD to be COLD and SUFFER.

And there was Sister Paul whose nose peeped out from the profile of her veil like that of a little pig. Dropping her sheets of music before she played the piano out of tune. Slightly comic always.

Another sister used to teach French and sing in a sweet, tiny voice. Not hard or gentle, and a mole sprouting hair on her chin.

Sisters of Truth in a day of long corridors with crosses

at the end. Mass, benediction, getting up cold and early, alone in bed. And the only man in their lives: the father who came to prepare flesh and blood in a chalice.

And the church bell rings on the hill, and the deaf man cannot hear it, and the nuns never kiss another's lips although he can read them.

AND SIFTING THROUGH THE SHARPENED PIECES OF MY VISION WHICH CHANGES WITH EACH NEW LIGHT, I HOLD A COLOURED FRAGMENT TO MY EYE AND SEE AGAIN ERNEST WITH HIS LONG, GREY BEARD AND HAIR, LIKE WILLIAM BLAKE SITTING IN A SOHO COFFEE BAR WITH HIS BAG OF BOOKS ON ASTROLOGY.

He had a leather coat down past his knees, and lived in the street. He almost knew who was going to come and consult him about their future by reading his own stars.

Believing in the effects of Mars, Mercury, Jupiter and the Moon on our city lives, he walked upon many nights down to Fleet Street to sit in an all night café. Down by Trafalgar Square and turn left into the Strand and right along until you see that sloping, grey street that never sleeps and lies awake waiting for tragedy.

When they turned him out of the Wimpy he worked from another coffee bar. This in a basement with a juke box. He put up a little cardboard sign with a photograph of himself with a girl from a pop group who had been to see him. He accepted cigarettes as though he were doing something naughty, and always coughed.

The noise from the juke box which was constantly in use irritated him. There was one record they played over and over again, the sprawling boys, and the girls who came down there alone and spoke to anyone. There was one record they played over and over again and he could never quite catch the words.

Once he was going down Oxford Street on a spring Friday afternoon, blown by the wind. He smiled shyly and didn't recognise us at first.

He wrote very neatly on sheets of blue notepaper when he worked out a horoscope. He charged five shillings and would accept a cheque.

I SEE PEOPLE BUILDING CITIES OF GLASS AROUND THEMSELVES. SMILING AS IF THEIR FACES WERE MADE OF GLASS AND IT WOULD CRACK. AND THE TEARS I CRY TURN TO PIECES OF GLASS BEFORE I HAVE CRIED THEM, AND I WEAR THEM STUCK TO MY CLOTHES LIKE MEDALS. AND THEY ONLY SHINE FOR SOME.

And I say, wishing I could say differently, live with him and he will become your warder. He has an invisible key to lock up your laughter, and his unseeing eyes will hypnotise you so that you can only respond to his television jokes.

You will know that he cannot bring you to life, although he feeds you with all kinds of soup and stew—bread and water to dry up your imagination.

He polishes his brown boots until he can see his face in them, but it is impossible to put the slightest shine in his eyes with poetry.

He will get you so that you are as disorganised to eternity as he is. You will be up at seven, have lunch at one, sweep the carpet, and turn on the television in time for the news at six. He will stop you from thinking further than the rent, and you will write nothing more interesting in your memory than cheque books.

At twenty-three he lives with his head under a gravestone. To be with him is to wear white for mourning.

MADNESS LOCKED INSIDE HIM; THE BRIGHTEST STAR IN THE SKY, SIRIUS, FASCINATED HIM. AT ONE TIME HE WAS WRITING A BOOK CALLED AFTER THE STAR.

Like the bright star, mirrors and window-panes full of stars taunted him. Deceptive and fragile, he found his release in smashing them. Everywhere he lived he smashed a window, this tall youth as naked as the grey boy who stands above the traffic at Hyde Park.

His eyes were as vulnerable as two blue windows that people could so easily smash with their thoughts and actions. People worried him.

He loved the graceful way she-cats moved, how tom cats prowled—outcasts like himself, he must have thought.

The trees, he said, were sometimes beckoning to him. He was always noticing the sky. How it changed colour. Standing still in the streets to watch, while others hurried by.

Wandering through a maze of uncomfortable furnished rooms. Pinning newspapers over yellow, faded surfaces to break the boredom of the walls. The rooms were so small and nasty that the best thing was to go to bed and sleep. To hide in sleep.

He came down the steps on winter or summer mornings and became a shepherd with a sailor's walk as he had love affairs with open spaces; shattered mirror puddles with his feet; and breathed in the fresh air so deeply that it made him dizzy.

Sometimes he drank from jam jars and ate eggs from

newspapers on the floor. But he was a prince and beggar of a world of his own making.

Some people said: 'He must be the HAPPIEST person in the world!' They heard him singing as he strode along. Others, who had seen his other side, hated him. To them he was a mountain of rage and egotism with his booming voice and actorly gestures. For sometimes every word was four-lettered. Yet sometimes he was gentle as a child, and kind. He'd run and fetch and carry for you, just like a child, to please.

He went to prison for a month because he couldn't cope with his desperate insecurity. He identified with his girlfriend, and hurt her, and all that was around her. She was SAD.

He wrote letters in which he said: 'At first I became sentimental and missed seeing the sky, but there are others in here far worse off than me.'

He was full of remorse. He looked different after they had cut off all his hair.

AN ALARM CLOCK AWAKES ME TO MANUFACTURED REALITY AND I SEE A MAN IN PYJAMAS, BEWILDERED, SCRATCHING HIS HEAD, FOR HE LIVES THE SAME DAY EVERY DAY. A routine day. A day of worries coming down like darkness.

He worries for everyone and everything. Cruel because he is kind and worshipper of hot dinners and well-made beds, and yet not a man who enjoys comfort himself. He can't relax in an armchair. Prefers a hard chair. Gets up early and goes to bed when others want to stay.

Busy as a bee he makes no honey for himself, but his bank manager regards him as an honest man. He never buys or gives on credit.

Often he ponders on death, about dying, about going

not to exist again. 'What's it all for?' he asks. And never dares to find an answer.

He has never failed in his duty, except that he has never failed in his duty. His only failure is that he has never been carefree.

His mother knitted. She knitted socks and dressing gowns of bright colours that didn't match from many spare balls of wool. She baked cakes with robins on at Christmas and jam tarts for children. She sniffed and drank gin when her husband died early. She had coils of grey hair that she couldn't comb when rheumatism gobbled up her fingers, and she had to be helped. She had a pearl hanging from her nose. She was a tall woman in black and maroon with bandy legs in thick stockings. She bought her first coffee stall with her wedding ring.

Son became a kind of husband to this woman out of a Victorian cameo and carried the responsibility of his father's death. His real wife found a saviour in his security, but lost a poet who might have been waiting somewhere.

SITTING NOW WAIST-DEEP IN GLASS, PIECES OF IT DROPPING AT ME FROM THE SKY, I FEEL TIRED AS I TRY TO REMAKE THE SURFACES WITH THINKING. AND THEN A THOUGHT COMES OUT LIKE THE SUN AND MAKES ME HAPPY, FOR IT GOES LIKE THIS . . .

Sammy has one thing. Sammy has a black face and teeth like polished chalks. Sammy has a lithe body. Sammy can dance.

He dances as if he were weaving a silver fishing net. As he moves limb and moves limb, he seems to be tacking the stitches all around the walls, embroidering the ceiling. Bathing us in light as he moves.

Sammy has boots of joy tacked to his black feet. He knows the air around him, he can catch it in his fingers. Sammy just smiles. Sammy just dances.

A golliwog with rubber limbs chasing shadows that he makes on the floor. A step ahead he dances, conjuring and turning others into cardboard cut-outs. Tops can't spin anymore when he pirouettes.

Yellow waistcoat and shining boots of joy, shining skin, shining teeth. Dance while we stand still, Sammy, gaping. Dance faraway from your tropical birds and sun. Dance your ballet that has jewels in it. Throw us coconuts full of warm milk, as you skip like a flame. Lend us some light. Sammy.

YES! I CLIMB THE GLASS STEPS TO AFFINITY WITH SAMMY, AND HE JUMPS SUDDENLY AWAY ON A CLOUD, AND SPINS ON ONE FOOT UNTIL HE MELTS LIKE A DREAM INTO THE CUMULUS. THEN GAZING BACK, ELATED, I SEE, FURTHER DOWN THIS MIRACULOUS STAIRCASE, ANOTHER IN NEED OF A HELPING HAND TO THE STARS.

See him, a statue in the flesh. A Greek God with olive skin, left over from the Parthenon. A Colossus in braces and City suit with muscles making lumps and bumps underneath. 'The body beautiful,' he says, drinking in his words like most people inhale cigarette smoke, 'The body beautiful has always been my aim.'

He will take from the drawer of his desk photographs of himself at eighteen entering the Mr Universe contest. And you will look from the face of black and white to the face by you and see that twenty years have shown little. And for the more daring there are pictures of him with girls on each shoulder, at the naturist camp, leaping around among the bracken as naked as when he came tumbling from a mortal's womb.

Consult him about vitamins and health foods and he will tell you all. He doesn't drink or smoke but carries a City umbrella which he swings as he strides like Tarzan through Mayfair.

He believes he is a bore when he talks too much about health and bodies, and his bachelorhood weighs heavily upon him.

Exceedingly well-mannered and boyish, he abhors bad language. 'Anglo-Saxon is for love-making,' he says. But somehow it is hard to imagine him using any but polite terms even among pillows.

He has the quality of the elephant boy about him and invisibly the jungle steams around his head as he works late in his office where it is very peaceful and people come to break their tension.

Try him on any subject and he will manage to trick you into a talk about sex. He discusses it clinically in detail and will invite you to join him in the skin for a healthy weekend and perhaps a game of tennis.

As well as photographs he has cheese and apples and milk tucked into his drawer. He is very kind and serious. He likes photography, taking pictures himself. Even when it's snowing he persuades models down to the camp and photographs the naked girls, naked himself except for his camera. He is very much a gentleman and will insist on taking them out to dinner afterwards.

Few people give him more than one thought.

Maybe one day he will rip off his City suit and lay down

his umbrella on an altar, and stride through Mayfair with his body beautiful blazing in the sun.

WHAT A CONTRAST IS THE MAN WHO OCCUPIES THE OFFICE BELOW HIM, WHO SMOKES CIGARS FROM ONYX ASHTRAYS AND WAVES A LARGE ONYX LIGHTER AS HE SITS BEHIND THE DESK THAT MAKES HIM A DWARF.

Fat of hand and face with large fish-blue eyes. Concentrating on making money and hiding behind an image that no one believes in of being a literary man who writes musicals and honesty.

He has a huge television set in his office and a cocktail cabinet and makes love to women on the floor. Unhappily married he spends more time away than at home and keeps mistresses.

He won't put up your wages but he'll woo you with promises, and then spend the week-end on his yacht. A little toy man on a wooden boat in a tub of bath water.

DABBLING MY HAND INTO THE SOAPY WATER, I SCOOP SOME UP TO SPLASH IN HIS FACE. REALISING THAT IT HAS TURNED TO SHARP PIECES IN MY HAND, I SEE HIM HASTILY PADDLING HIS TUB AWAY WITH A BATH BRUSH, FULLY DRESSED.

AND AS HE IS SWEPT AWAY BY A HUGE WAVE OF POUND NOTES, I TRY NOT TO CARE ABOUT HIM AND OTHERS LIKE HIM. AND PICKING UP A PIECE OF GLASS THAT HAS NOT SPLINTERED WITH THE REST, I LOOK AGAIN AND SEE ANOTHER FIGURE COMING TOWARDS ME, WALKING A LITTLE HIGHER THAN THE PAVEMENTS WITH A BOOK TUCKED UNDER HIS ARM. PRAISE HIM!

The wind blows back his dark, curly hair from his forehead and a scarf wound round his neck could never strangle his adventures. Behold him, the young adventurer, delving into mysteries that he finds in places that others ignore as ordinary.

One evening he was chatting to a toothless old hag who feeds the birds in squares. He found her, this piece of human rubbish, discarded by the world, going through the garbage, sifting out the wasted food from the papers and pieces of glass. She stood with her baskets at her feet, filled by dustbin not supermarket, and told him marvellous stories about pigeons.

'There's Pegleg,' she said. 'He walks on two stumps. He lost his feet in the tar. They all have names.' She flew lightly from beak to feather to personality. He flew with her.

You will find him adventuring in all kinds of odd places with all kinds of people. Dipping his fingers into cesspools and bringing out gold.

For example, there was Lenny of the filing-cabinet mind. Out of each pocket came a press-cutting neatly folded. Each sentence rippled with data unpunctuated by breaths because he had to get it all out so quickly. A river poured from his mouth and if you weren't very careful he could drown you and you'd have to go outside to gasp for air. An expert on human abnormalities, he could pick them out from a crowd like Ernest picked stars from the sky.

Darting around, buzzing with thoughts, tumbling with sentences, looking for matches in empty boxes. Worrying. In his speeded-up world haunting dives while others sleep. Waking from dreams which end with someone crying. Remembering even his dreams in detail.

Lenny full of kindness who talked too much. Lenny who liked young boys too much and became a slave to the shrewd ones who came down from the North and anointed themselves rulers of his flat with smelly drains outside the window, and no throne, only a cupboard flooding from floor to ceiling with magazines.

Lenny, hooked on young boys, experimented with nearly every drug and never got hooked. He wrote a drug play for adolescents, teaching them that pills only bring one down, to earth. Addicts made their home with him too. And he even had to move for fear of the police finding the needles and syringes they took three meals a day with.

He was also writing a play about L.S.D.—how a young mod gets high on it and the whole city comes to him like visions on a stage. Someone said the appropriate setting for it was a cathedral.

This was Lenny, only one of those the young adventurer delighted in, and then moved on because the street signs pointed away.

There was another—a tall, splay-footed, dreamy-eyed, man-boy in a flower-strewn shirt. Day-in, day-out he was blocked and got everything, but didn't when he couldn't score which was a pity. They went to clubs and dug the sounds. But after a while the music-magic seemed to stop and the adventurer went on, alone, because somewhere a flute was playing for him.

See him wandering around bookshops as if he were in Paradise already, and slipping a book under his coat as skilfully as Jean Genet, when broke, but not broken. Praise him for such stealing.

He has learnt what women are and they miss the things he teaches them when he goes.

He has a lot to give as he walks a little higher than the pavements turning the streets into a fairground with his eyes. And although he sometimes cannot quite understand the jingle-jangle and the bells, he senses something important. He knows his journey has no ending but he's moving in the right direction.

NOW AS SHE WAS THEN I SEE HER IN A SHELTERED WORLD SURROUNDED BY FEAR. She lives a dream in the tiny office as she smokes her weeks away with countless cigarettes.

She dreams she is a foreign correspondent as she tours her suburban district in the car that her parents bought her. Their only child, clinging to her childhood still.

She has seen many come and many go, and she goes on, getting out the newspaper as the days pass in Linotype and the newspaper blows from the counter to tell soggy lies in the gutter.

There is no love in her life; no physical purely lusty lovely love. Instead she does good deeds and buys toys for other people's children. She hates to be touched and believes it's wicked, although she is well-read and travels the race courses with her massive, amoeba-like father. She once said in confidence that a boy she went out with touched her breast, that she enjoyed it. It must never happen again. Enlightened in all, she says: 'Unmarried people shouldn't make love in any circumstances, unless of course He's going to war and She might never see him again.'

What fruitful, fruitless nicotined days she leaves behind with the lines of copy. She is making no news herself and her ash-filled typewriter may as well be silent.

THERE'S ALSO A GIRL LIKE A HELTER-SKELTER. Round and round she goes taking you with her in a spin. A hectic living girl with humour who can live with dust under the bed and under her nose without noticing.

Her cooking is slipshod and she boils up fish and slings it on a tin plate steaming, for the cat who has only half a tail.

What a nice girl she is. She is like a Peter Pan. She won't wear stockings often and doesn't care about ladders when she does, for boys still run their fingers up her legs for she's got something else that's not synthetic.

She is constantly on some course at college, with paint sticking to her handbag and tea-rings on her sketching. She likes neat boys who stick their hearts to her like jam tarts. After eating them hurriedly and enjoying the taste while it lasts, she slips away tip-toe like the Knave.

Her father is the same shape of person, a crazy Welshman who fitted loudspeakers all over the rambling house, and has a whole room of dusty tapes. He pulled down the kitchen wall and never put it back again because he forgot. And then he went off to Scotland to look after delinquent boys with his placid wife who has eyes as big as saucers.

He never finished anything but never noticed the cracks in the lavatory pan or the cobwebs on his ten hundred books. Never noticed he never noticed. To him his home is a castle although the windows are dirty and the garden overgrown. It is a Land of Song full of lodgers.

He has left his daughter to collect the rents and misbehave. She has a double-bed in the front room, always shared and untidy. She has geraniums in the gas-stove and buckets on the table. She washes her hair with the scrubbing brush and dries it on the tea towel.

She is a naughty Puck. She will remain an unevolved artist with her paint brush but she has already attained a higher state of self. The neighbours would not notice. They only notice the overflowing dustbin on the doorstep and prick up their ears hungrily at the noise.

AND OFTEN SEARCHING FOR AN ADVENTURE TO GO ON FOR MYSELF, I STOP PEOPLE TO ASK THE WAY, TO ASK QUESTIONS. THEY SHAKE THEIR HEADS AND SHRUG THEIR SHOULDERS AS IF PUZZLED BY MY REQUEST. AND AS A SUBSTITUTE FOR MAGIC HOLD OUT IN THEIR HANDS A PIECE OF SMOKED-GLASS.

Her bust billows and her hips are small and she cannot get dresses to fit without having them altered and has a struggle with herself to go shopping.

She has many books on the theatre, on the cinema, on all kinds of subjects and reads them, but appears to learn little about herself.

You can tell her the truth and she will not really listen because she has set a thought pattern and adheres to it rigidly.

'What will I do but wander and drift?' she asks the mirror which reveals her less attractive than she is. She will scorn at lace and frills, prefers hard-wearing underwear. She will not escape in froth and femininity.

She has had many lovers. She is not hard to get. She has touched many black, shining skins and given herself away.

'She cannot open herself,' a boy once said. 'A woman is a hole, she must know how to open herself.'

She gave herself in a forest when she was only fourteen,

to prove that she could. She has been proving she can ever since.

Often she cannot be bothered to be bothered. Looks like a healthy Russian peasant with rosy cheeks like apples when she chops fruit salad or washes up.

Her brother who is sixteen throws knives at a piece of wood and is thinking of getting a girlfriend. Their father died in a car crash. He used to go mountaineering. They knew he would die dangerously, but not so soon.

Their mother is silent and sincere and slightly chilled by death, and has settled down to being a woman alone, and likes paintings and being associated with associations.

They kept a junkie for a few days, who had a junkie wife. They caught him stealing the milk and yoghurt from the doorstep, and he could not recollect it. They helped him fix and bleed and cry, and were sorry.

WHAT DID HE HAVE TO OFFER BUT A PHOTOGRAPH OF LIFE? He came across the Iron Curtain shortly before they closed the Gate to the East and West. It is the most adventurous thing he has ever done. And now he sits and looks at me taking pictures in his mind all the time, unable to look at himself.

Wiry, Hungarian, healthy with hair showing through the V of his towelling shirt, and springy of step with rubber-soled shoes to keep him from slipping, he carries every type of equipment with him except that to protect his feelings. Organised into pockets, flaps and cases, are films, tripods, stands, slides and light gauges. He is the walking camera and can photograph all but what you're thinking.

From an isolated world and the hair receding from his forehead like dandelion feathers that tell the time, shyly he peers out, eyes yet pin-like and critical. He is the true Virgoan, obsessed by detail which blurs his vision.

His gloomy flat has a screened-off kitchen. On the screen a little notice says 'Do Not Disturb'—there are few disturbances.

There is a whole world on the walls carefully created at the Kodak factory. Bridges, houses, cats, umbrellas, beaches. And pretty girls look down from every angle. He goes home to his empty roomful of women, and they have eyes for everyone.

SOMEONE TOLD ME A STORY ABOUT A MAN OUT OF FOCUS, TWICE AS BIG AS LIFE, WHO TOOK SIZE TWELVE IN BOOTS. OR WAS IT TRUE?

He roared like a lion and laughed as if human and ate at the table long after others had finished.

He made fifteen children and loved many more women than one. He threw bottles through pub windows at closing time, went to the music halls, and when drunk tossed pennies in the air for children to scamper for and catch. And he'd drag his eldest daughter out of bed to play the piano.

Never ungenerous, broke he'd say, 'Sure you're all right for money dear?' and if you weren't, change all that. Yet he passed the ticket collectors with a victory sign. He never paid his fare to anywhere.

A good profession as a script writer cramped his style, so he became bookie, decorator, anything he fancied, and spent hours racing and making friends in the open air. He never missed porridge and haddock and duck eggs for breakfast and kept an old piece of lemon to flavour his tea.

When he spat in the grate it would come whizzing by your ear like silver to turn to treacle on the fender. He was a mighty man who loved cementing and bodging-up. He had an eldest son who was not quite as mighty—who bought a houseboat that the tide washed away.

He lived every moment until he was over eighty and even then they couldn't keep him down. His bedroom was called his study and he wouldn't allow anyone to dust it.

At Christmas King Henry came to dinner. He'd wipe the grease from his hands on the cat.

And when he died, so suddenly a frail man, they cremated him. His wife, reminded by the boots still kept polished under the dresser, couldn't believe in the little casket they gave her to put in the parlour. And after all this her hair, which she could sit on, hadn't gone grey.

Or so the story goes.

I PUT DOWN THE BOOK THAT IS THE PAST, AND GOING FOR A STROLL I FIND SUCH A LOVING, COOING COUPLE, WHOM I CAN SEE THROUGH AS CLEARLY AS GLASS. So open you cannot help loving their love. She sees him kingly although his crown appears to have toppled to one side and the tray they carry to the kitchen together bears no sceptre. They do everything together.

People come like lost babes in wooden boxes to their doorstep for they will help anyone with a problem but will not hesitate to list their weaknesses when they are gone.

Their world in one room is like a neat little dove-nest love-nest with a window-box where flowers flower; and when it's cold they grow inside among the furniture, in the cushion covers, between the cracks in their held hands which can never be welded.

Happy is their love and they will include yet exclude you. She will envy your eyes because hers are small, and talk emphatically about nipples. He will scold her for her foolishness and love her for the things she cannot see.

LOOK FOR WISDOM AMONG THE SPLINTERS AND PERHAPS YOU'LL FIND IT HERE? Here is where he has built his hermit's cave in a grim, four-storeyed house. In his room at the top he has completely revolutionised the day. He cooks eggs and bacon at two a.m. and sleeps in light. And when he feels inclined, throws his washing water from a bowl out of the window.

Intriguing you will find him because although he pretends stupidity he'll pick your wits with needles to confirm ideas he already has. And oh! what marvellous fantasies he has had time to invent.

Ill-health, a gammy leg, has kept him there for years. Alone he has passed his youth away. He slices the canvas uppers of his bumper boots to let his toes breathe, and safety-pins his trousers.

He sends strange cuttings through the post and reads the Standard from cover to cover and wonders.

They say he's lazy, that his leg is just an excuse for not working. But he's been through butchery in hospital wards. If it's purely laziness it must be a struggle to be lazy.

He chews each mouthful twenty times before he swallows. Sends the best Christmas cards out of the entire family, whom he rarely sees, and who never see him.

COME AND MEET AN ARTIST AND GET A DEEP, FRESH BREATH

OF FLESH OIL PAINT. Where he lives it is very quiet and full of something sacred. To sit before his fire on an autumn night is to be very happy while the kettle boils.

You will, however, note his selfishness which is acceptable in his case for he is unselfish with the part of him that he can spare, the part that doesn't go hot into the canvas he paints or the guitar he seduces with long-nailed fingers.

He is no recluse and unlike Gauguin has an efficient accountant.

Go button-buying in his car for a pearl button that is missing from his sage-green, military-style jacket, and it is a pleasant trip with imitations from behind the wheel of a motorist being thumped for careless driving. You see, not only can he do it through art but he can create through living in real life too.

He can hold you tightly and say that he loves you and has eyes brown like soft nuts to eat with your own eyes. But when he takes off his socks he has dirty toenails and it worries you. And he has just washed his hair.

It doesn't matter really because he is warm and full of something holy—being alive and aware. Whatever you do you will not stop his mind working or being fascinated by a shape or colour or the colour of a chord.

Make music with your artist while you can. He will not let you help him iron his shirts. He hates to be helped because he says tomorrow he will miss it. He doesn't want to be domesticated and too settled, but will scold you if you forget a saucer to match your cup for he likes everything to have a place. And to him a cup without a saucer is like a man without a woman. To him that is impossible.

SUCCESSFUL NOW, he winks at us like an uncle before

he faces seriously the small gathering of hangers-on who come to pick the crumbs from under his sumptuous table. Thinner than he was. His trousers hang around his bottom.

'We've booked a table for ten,' he says—at some 'in' restaurant. Then he looks at his watch and says he must hurry because he has to be at a lecture. A lecturer now he sees himself, talking about acting and success to those who have not tasted its bitter sweetness.

He'll show you proudly round his flat when he has time. He'll show you fine paintings and the bedroom with a three dimensional bed because his legs are extra long. He'll open cupboards and look contentedly at the rows of suedes and clean suits and polythene bags. 'That's one thing I enjoy now,' he'll say, 'having everything clean.' It wasn't clean where he came from, scraping sticks along the crumbling walls of his childhood, giving birth to this image.

Now he hails taxis and rides noticed through the traffic that never ceases. He talks of limousines and trips abroad. He has made it but never wants to stop working. He's discovered that stardom is less clean than the place his talent came from.

I REMEMBER MR EDWARDS WHOM CHILDREN RESPECT. PUTTING IMAGINATION BEFORE THE POINTLESS TRIANGLE AND INCORRECT GRAMMAR HE TEACHES LIKE FEW.

He came and dropped a pile of fairy stories on the doorstep when I was eight and ill in bed. Taught me how to hunt a monster called a Hippogriff in crumpled words on an inky exercise book.

He runs competitions giving away bars of chocolate for

poems and paintings and he understands what children mean in their essays.

Envy him in his classroom with faces of clowns and friezes on the wall. He has a wand not a whistle because he still believes in magic.

Envy him that he can perspire at the end of term when the children put on their play of 'Ali Baba And The Forty Thieves'. Envy that he worries about the scenery bumping and hurries away after the applause.

HE STANDS IN PURPLE AND DENIM WITH A CURTAIN OF SILVER FOR A SHAWL, AND TALKS OF LOVE AND L.S.D. Cardboard sandals tied to his feet and pink chiffon knotted to his neck. There's a gap where his two front teeth used to be.

Over the heath he goes laughing and leaping, tall in the lilac dusk. And an aeroplane tears a hole in the sky.

Sitting in the dew on his silver curtain, reflected in the sky in the pond, he tells a legend about how he took a trip and thought he saw a vision of a man riding a white horse. But it wasn't a vision it was real and the policeman on the horse said, 'What are you doing here?' Amazed by it all he simply replied, 'Man, what a beautiful horse you have. What a beautiful horse!' And the policeman smiled and now a knight galloped away into the night that was no longer starless.

He tosses a bottle of lemonade to his lips, throws stones and blows his nose on a leaf. Pretends he's a statue on a wall and a maniac crouching in a bush. Wants to go to the fun-fair that's locked.

And later, on the platform where silver trains crash in, he shows the colours of his topaz ring in the softness of a match. He has a ring on every finger.

Then he floats away on a silver bird reading a nursery comic and doesn't worry about where he's going.

SOMEONE PRODDING MAKES ME JUMP. IT IS MRS PRINGLE AND I HAVE MISLAID THE KEY TO THE FILING CABINET WHERE SHE LOCKS UP HER DREAMS.

Mrs Pringle has a son who's a talented musician who is doing well as a trainee bank clerk. He saved £100 last year. He has one hundred pounds in the bank. Mrs Pringle is very proud of Alec her son. More her son than her husband's son. They share little jokes together.

You are very respectable Mrs Pringle. You were in the W.R.N.S. You married your husband two years after you met. You had turned him down on many occasions for other more attractive dates. Does he love you Mrs Pringle?

Why is it Mrs Pringle that it appears that you are making-up to the men who come in, that you are winking at them behind your glasses and nice clean skin? No, you are very respectable Mrs Pringle. Have you not said that you can't stand people to show each other affection in public?

You have plump, calfy legs Mrs Pringle and well-repaired shoes. You like brooches that glitter and shopping bags with zips. You bring two chocolate biscuits to have with your morning cup of tea. You lead the conversation at tea time. You talk about frozen macaroni puddings and Surprise garden peas. Has nothing ever surprised YOU Mrs Pringle?

Oh Mrs Pringle why is it you're so nice to everyone? So chatty? And you could teach us all such lessons Mrs Pringle about facts and figures and how to spring-clean the carpets with soap powder. You reveal such mysteries each time you speak. How you braise your meat on Saturday. How Alec doesn't like gravy.

You have bought a new second-hand car Mrs Pringle. It's a sort of dirty mustard. You paid outright for it. It needs some wing mirrors. You say Mrs Pringle that it took your last penny, that you had to go without at week-ends to pay the last bit. But you say: 'Take care of the pennies and the pounds take care of themselves. And I always have a little in reserve that I don't like to think about.'

You are very proud to say you know where every penny goes.

Your mother lives in Bishop's Stortford and you have friends there who live in Pig Lane. You think that really is funny because the houses in Pig Lane are big and modern. Your father likes pork chops, two at a time.

You say Mrs Pringle that your brother is always pleading poverty and yet takes four holidays a year. When he went to Bournemouth in the summer he phoned every night to say what was on the menu.

You went to Italy and Austria for your holiday. You weren't very impressed.

You're always very accurate. You have an adding machine on your desk. But you say your head adds up quicker. You have a very alert brain. The machine makes you impatient.

You take your adding machine, pencils and books off the desk and put them on the cupboard at night so that the cleaner will not forget to dust.

You love housework. Don't you Mrs Pringle? You really love housework. You said how much you really love housework. Didn't you?

Who are you?

TO SAVE MYSELF FROM BEING ECLIPSED BY MRS PRINGLE'S NAMELESS SHADOW, I RUN AS FAST AS MY LEGS WILL CARRY ME THROUGH AN UNLABELLED DOORWAY and find I am in a classroom where students cannot use razor blades or knives, and the adjoining lavatory has a door you can see head-over and legs-under.

This classroom has SEX painted on the woodwork in bright yellow. One of the exhibits has 'PLEASE DO NOT DRAW LADIES' VAGINAS' scrawled on it.

There is a man in the corner with a worn shirt collar who dribbles and jerks his limbs and head, and communicates in a gutteral language of his own invention.

Another stands in the centre doing a self-portrait from a mirror. A huge man in a baggy suit, with black hair that seems almost to stand on end with his intensity. As he paints, the sweat breaks out on his forehead in glistening diamonds. He goes outside leaving a strange, beautifully drawn face on the easel—a similar one is already hanging on the wall. And he wipes away the diamonds into his handkerchief before he returns.

Fred, with a hooked nose, who keeps insisting he isn't Jewish, wears owl-like spectacles and has a very high forehead and hair like a crow's feathers. His trousers are far too long but he refuses to alter them and turns them up at the bottom considerably instead. And he picks flowers called Dog-ends that grow on the parquet and puts them neatly into a tin. He dramatises the cough they give him but shrugs his shoulders. 'What else can I do on ten bob a week pocket money?' he says.

He switches from being very uppercrust to being very coarse. Talks in detail of his war wounds. 'My trouble is women,' he says. 'I'm very jealous. I can't share a woman.'

He sells saccharine tablets at a penny a time to other patients; and appears to make a small profit out of anything. He keeps re-arranging chairs and tables and moving a vase of flowers and sweeping the floor noisily.

'There he's doing it again!' shouts a flabby man in his late twenties with short sleeves and fat arms folded. A pig-like face. A face people detest on sight.

'The world's a cesspool,' he says in an American drawl. 'Yes I'm a pessimist.' He talks almost obscenely about the effects of a nuclear war.

Someone whistles and he shouts again: 'I'll smash you if you don't stop that!' But he doesn't move and won't because as he explains, 'I'm a voluntary patient.'

A distinguished, middle-aged man with grey hair and a sun-tan hands over a little booklet called *Thought For The Day*; it's his bible; it tells how to live one day at a time, positively and harmoniously. He is an alcoholic. His wife and children were killed in a car crash, he says. He says people are as big as the things that get them down.

Later, a West Indian male nurse in a crisp, white jacket, who looks as if he belongs behind an expresso bar, says: 'He's a liar. He's a psychopath. The wife and children are a myth!'

But the staff eat plump tomatoes and tasty pies while patients make-do.

Fred suddenly holds up an enormous pair of men's pants. 'Are they yours miss?' he asks. She threatens to send him back to the ward.

Nicky, an aesthetic boy, who is schizophrenic and has a wife and three children, paints alone on a large piece of hardboard. He is beautiful but sometimes finds the simplest decision impossible.

A woman with an affected voice and a double-barrelled

name comes to the class giving the impression that she is taking part in a play. She wears a shabby skirt and a jacket and black casual shoes with soles laughing where they have come unstitched. Her hands are young. Her sad eyes are of a girl. Her complexion flakes. Her shaggy, grey hair falls in straight lines over her shoulders.

She says she didn't want to come. Sits down and paints. She paints two daffodils. She paints a tree and two birds flying in opposite directions. She paints a bottle of wine and a glass. All two things separated.

'Quite puts you off,' she murmurs with a disdainful look at Fred who is drawing aeroplanes with a biro. Someone offers her a Woodbine. 'I can smoke any cigarette but these,' she says. 'No, I'm not married. One of the doctors thought I should get married. Someone to look after me, he said. I'd never really thought about it like that before. I couldn't stand the idea of marriage. Now I'm considering it.'

There is a little Indian man with a face as pure as a saint's, wearing a suedette coat with a fur collar and a trilby hat which he lifts from his head. His eyes are brown candlelight. He talks about a universal religion and has a pile of drawings and paintings to illustrate his ideas. He is torn between his strict upbringing and what he believes in. He can read palms, is gentle, and is going to a monastery one day to be a yogi.

A junkie, an Australian with hip ways, comes in from the river. 'I've dropped in for a minute. I've come home to pick up some jeans.'

He's working at a boat-yard and is the energy force of the hospital. His folder reveals fabulous crayon drawings—shapes like brightly coloured flames moulded into faces and a crucifixion. And there is a drawing of a negro girl in very tight pants, naked to the waist, twisting like a snake in front of her mirror.

A youth with a sullen face and split jeans walks around in circles. He resents being asked questions.

'You sound like the doctor,' he says.

And an old man in a check cap and black boots works like a neat cobbler on a sketchbook, all by himself, painstakingly.

TURNING AWAY FROM THESE PORTRAITS WHICH ARE PAINTED BY THE WORLD, THE YOUNG ADVENTURER TAKES ME BY THE ARM, AND SAYS, I THINK YOU OUGHT TO LOOK AT THIS NOW. AND I SAY, YES, ANYTHING.

We go down worn-down star-steps into the world that is a club. They take your coat and stick a tab on it at three in the morning. The air is black-black and heavy with uplifting life, and it sings: 'Come and cleanse yourselves in me little children.'

And ebony boys with simple minds dance in spotlights of their own creation before the primeval dawn. And Love gropes over the floorboards which are floating in a fantasy and anchored only to the eye.

AND THOSE WHO DON'T BELONG BELONG BECAUSE THEY DON'T BELONG AND NOBODY BELONGS AND YET BELONGS AS THE SHINING MUSIC THROBS US INTO BEING MORE THAN WE BELIEVE.

From the ceiling of the sky a huge, glittering mirror-ball hangs, reflecting only what it sees and seas, and ever-changing as it moves the same endless, smooth, sharp-cornered circle. And the glass ball in the ceiling that has no stars, winks and waits and goes on turning and never waits. And with the steady, sure, uncertain increase of unseen speed, in turning only sensing and guessing, and knowing sometimes, and knowing more, I see them all again—the people—fragments of an ecstacy, skipping with ropes of lead and blowing me kisses of glass that will remain.

AND MY HEART IS MADE OF GLASS AND BREAKS. AND I MEND MY HEART MYSELF.
AND STANDING A LONG WAY OFF, BUT VERY NEAR, I SEE . . .

Poet with his ringleted, standing-on-end hair. Understood, misunderstood, denied as phoney.

Poet and musician with music words and music that speaks like a field of Van Gogh's flowers. Soft suede jacket and goblin shoes and trousers with stripes. Mystery behind your dark glasses that attempt to hide your ancient, dead, young, alive eyes.

Found your true voice you have. Said the things that will stay said. Humbled yourself before humanity and kept your pride.

Your aura is full of the perfume of hashish, of slaps in the face with metal hands, and nights that are lived till morning, and the laughter of someone who knows he need find no answer.

Little boy like; needing the breast still; leader dominating the scene and influencing the mind like the wind touches the sea while no one is looking; commanding with your giggles and silences; kicking your small heels up and dancing; waving your arms around and going further than the present.

Sharing secrets with few, though sharing all, and lucky

enough to be separated from time and travel.

Followed by your men like Robin Hood; men in shades and floral shirts and white shoes, not Lincoln Green. Vulnerable though protected by so much and many. Wandering in starry places with foetus still upon you.

Follow him through the scented clouds that will harm only the unseeing and those who have nothing else.

Follow him, clinging on to his heartbeats.

YOU WRITE ME A LETTER FROM KUWAIT.

YOU HAVE BECOME A CHARACTER IN A BOOK TO ME; A KEROUAC; A MAILER; A YOUNGER HENRY MILLER. WE HAVE WRITTEN YOU INTO A BOOK BETWEEN US; AN EVER-LIVING BOOK WHICH ENDS AS SOON AS I CHOOSE TO CLOSE THE MEMORIES THAT BIND IT, AND IT BEGINS AGAIN IN BEAUTIFUL SPIRITUAL PARAGRAPHS THAT I CONTINUE TO FEED UPON.

YOU SAY YOU ARE NOT COMING BACK FOR A LONG TIME. YOU ARE GOING INTO EGYPT; DOWN INTO SPAIN; UP INTO SWEDEN. YOU SAY YOU ARE LOCKED-UP AGAIN, BUT NOT FOR LONG. YOU ARE MORE OPTIMISTIC ABOUT IT THAN BEFORE. YOU STOLE SOME CANVAS TO MAKE A TENT. WHY NOT?

YOU SAY, WHEN YOU REALISE THAT YOU COULD HAVE DONE ALL THIS BEFORE, THIS TRAVELLING, YOU COULD KILL YOURSELF. YOU SUGGEST THAT MAYBE I'LL JOIN YOU IN PARIS OR BRUSSELS WHEN IT'S WARMER. BUT I WILL NEVER COME, ALTHOUGH I AM WITH YOU, HIKING THROUGH HOT AND COLD, FLOATING SHADOW-CONTINENTS, TOWARDS INFINITY. AMONG A MILLION SUNS.

YES, YOU HAVE KILLED US AND I HAVE KILLED YOU. NOW WE ARE ALIVE, ETERNALLY IN EACH OTHER'S ARMS, THOUGH NEVER TOUCHING OR SEEING, FOR NOTHING THAT REALLY <u>IS</u> IS EVER <u>WAS</u>.

BETWEEN THE BROKEN GLASS OF US, OF EVERYTHING, THE PEOPLE PLAY. AND I PLAY WITH THEM, FOR BROKEN GLASS STILL SHINES.

Lyman Andrews

THE DEATH OF MAYAKOVSKY

and other poems

FOR PIERRE EMMANUEL AND
JACK AND CATHERINE LAMBERT

Grateful acknowledgements are due to the following periodicals in which many of these poems first appeared: *Adam International Review, El Corno Emplumado, Evergreen Review, Fishpaste, In Particular, New Mexico Quarterly, Stand, Transatlantic Review,* and to the Lorrimer Press.

The Death of Mayakovsky
(for P.H.J. and C.P.S.)

I

(when he died
he crept out of his body
into the poem in his pocket)

2

Look there!
the old woman
hasn't got any shoes

wearing a red kerchief
she sweeps
white snow from a black street

you put
your best poster
into her rough hand

she stops sweeping
to watch you
fly off down the street

poems hopping
from your pockets
a red poppy springing from your head

3
Verdigris
clogs the machines

Workers
shine rows of fat bullets

(flutes and balalaikas
weave patterns on ash)

4
Dragging
your bursting bag of images

you would enter
a smoky room

insane metaphors
with a logic all their own

sprouted from your tongue

your hands described
a geometry of invisible graftings

steel girders
and hearts on fire

concrete chessboards
and 150,000,000 individuals

crazy geometry!

black bread and vodka
ideals and realities of flesh

the geography
of naked bodies

celebrations
of numbers & flowers

forests where trees move like men

railways disappearing
through fields of algebra

lakes and pines and darkness
cold emptiness

you hammered logic from chaos

you were Namer of Things
you tried to become God

5

It's terrible
these banners flying
sparkling red in the sun

it's terrible
the posters
with gentle eyes

blood crawls slowly
bone shines through flesh
you lean against a fish-oil lamp

impersonal shadows on walls
papers in locked files
friendly warnings

you become translucent
you wither in the desks of editors
you are an image

you have no reality
you are an improbable creation of yourself
you are nobody

under the sparkling banners
the gentle-eyed posters
deny you

6
Through the cold streets
Night stretches out dark fingers

She draws in the light
exchanging it for a subtler pattern

Over the streetlamps, moths
weave filigrees

You remove them from the air
gently

and touch them to the page

7
Mayakovsky!
help the anti-poets
nail the poets to the sky!
wake them
from their dreams of hot flesh and garters
crumble thunderclouds
between your palms
let naked children collect
spilt coins of the sun
and broken bits of the moon
let the stunned audiences wait forever
for the descent of Nijinski
send butterflies to the pesthouse
to smear honey
on crusted lips
pity the old men
lost in arctics of white
pluck
the last flower of agony
but above all
Mayakovsky
spit on
the elegant poet
who yawns, squeezes himself
and lets drop
into an enamelled box
one tiny, ornate
scream
saving his protest
a voyeur
with a wrinkled condom

8
(Deep
where a cold sun sifts
through dark forests
through loam and hidden rivers
where pine needles a foot thick
soften the flinty earth

There the North Wind
cracks trees
with pistol shots
and great Georgian swans
weave bright flowers in their wings
for your death)

9

No longer does the poem
JUMP OUT
and pretend to be a
CHAIR
h i
a a
i h
r c
t u m b
r l
o e
l i k e
a r o b
n c a
a t
or become
a glass of water
s u
p s o
o r y
u p u
t r o d
i i l n
n s o i
g c h
m e
a b
t
i p
c u
but like a TIGER, it
c r e e p s

BITES off your
HEAD

(and runs away with you
inside)

10

Banners fly!

Men are shot!
Mouths fill with lime

Poems are burnt!

(spring rains
filled your skull with ashes

it was time to become a cloud with trousers)

11

Pain became confused
with the poem
the skull ached

a flower
unfurled
behind your eyes

was it
pain
or a poem?

your skull exploded

12

If you *did* get to heaven
Vladimir Vladimirovich, do you watch the sea

dazzling
foam-fractured green

wave across clouds
to your comrades

or yell and toss your cap

and collide with ascending bureaucrats

to watch them float back
into the sea

fat men
on leaky rubber tyres

or do you just
row your mad cloud across the sky

drink contraband vodka
and smoke foggy cigarettes

dropping ashes like lilac petals
on Brooklyn Bridge

The Invalid

You wouldn't say
the family didn't want
her, only

She never said a word.
Old and feeble
she lay

Picking at the quilt
in her room
(that smelled

Or so the family said
of wet wool and urine).
A cat

Leapt in the window
from a tree now and then
and was fed

Bits by the old woman
from a cracked white
saucer

They always served her tea
on. Days passed
as they always do

Until she no longer
knew the cat
or bothered to feed it.

This is what she lived
a neutral-plastered room
containing

A bed with horsehair mattress
table, chair. And her,
surrounded

By the family down-
stairs unnoticed as
the air.

From time to time
the family was tempted
to send her away for

Proper care. Unsure
they talked things
over

When somehow she
heard, somehow
a spark caught

Her poor lump of a mind
and one morning
early

She got downstairs
to the kitchen, turned
on the gas

And folded her hands. She
never said a word
to anyone.

But in her room was
a note carefully
written in a shaky hand:

It's no good to be alone.

Le Monde sans Arme (for Martin Luther King)

a dove
a yellow sun
& green branch

paper the colour of cream

that's all
not enough after all

a taste of oil
thick air
dark Northern clouds

a sheriff with sagging gun

wax candles
in coloured light

water in a stone bowl

John the Baptist
holding in two cupped hands
his severed head

is it raining in Memphis

Paris unfolding
like a Japanese flower
in water

gum-chewing pilgrims

the great Rose illumination
    shatters
    on old stone

'we've killed one more poor
nigger'

sunlight on ancient stone
cafes
full of flashing kids

so easy to forget to hate

squatting toads
    a pack of greasy cards
    blue thick air

I am the Negro's killer

concrete officials
littering the squares
proud blood-stained ribbons

'those goddamn niggers'

my ears
stuffed full of Bach
my mind
a rat-heap of images
from some seedy carnival of poetry

lazy river in a lazy sun

tell me the poem
I can show the Negro child
whose stomach
    flowers
    into brilliance
    from a .38

opaque & white
the dove's blind eyes

in this easy foreign sunshine
I hear jackboots trampling
    music
    flowers
    images

poor bloody ruined corpse

one April day in Paris
when I learn again how it feels
to be American

Icarus

Icarus, his hair
crackling like thunder,
stood first on one leg
then on the other, trembling
at his father's touch
as the great wings were fitted
with strong bands of leather
across the narrow breast.
His feet quivered
and his heart jerked
with the young excitement
that leaves the bowels hollow,
until at last the wings
were on, and Daedalus stood
and said: these wings were made
for our escape; and frowned
a warning at his son
who couldn't hear a word.
Icarus plunged head down
into the shining air
and soaring, diving, rising,
he rinsed himself of those
old terrors of earth, clay,
and metallic deaths:
but the sea glittered
with the strewn fragments
of the sun, and
the heat, white-hot
as new hammerleavings,
stirred the wax to liquid
in the wings, until

the boy, Icarus
seeing feathers break-
ing free, struggled harder
and found he was not frightened
but feeling godlike
and in that blinding moment
he made his last, noble
effort, ignored the shout
of Daedalus, and sprang
still higher, until
his sweat sizzled
gashes broke red (bright coals)
through the charred crust
of his rib-cage
and then
            only
                  ashes
falling like blackbirds
to the waiting sea

Vous Savez Vous Savez

1
That, on the wood
bench turning
the colour
of old violins

he sits, he
sits though all
over the
place, pigeons

& butterflies
fracture
the watery
light

into old
photographs
new
memories

2
better think
where

to walk
ignore

this clown
ignore

the sadness
in his zinc

eyes
wondering froggily

where
went all the

skyrockets
& roses

3
you should
know, you
know

enough
to hear the
cracking

the awful
crazing
of his skull

under
that funny
hat

Two Poems

I

Nothing is ever
free, you said

yes,
even in poems

whether only
of a dog

in the rain
(look

in her eyes)
or of cold

grapes
in a glazed bowl

perception
is difficult

takes it
out of you

like any act of will
or love.

2

Sweet
pools of shadow

blurring
the hard line of the bed

where I taste your sweat
on the pillow

touch your bent
dark head, asleep—

there's not much left
finally

except to
believe in grace

Pierrot

When they arrested him
a white ring of toothpaste
around his mouth
made him look like
a badly painted doll
whose expression of surprise
was overdone

When they tried him
he didn't say anything at all
but rubbed one finger
along the polished wooden rail
and when the verdict came
his expression of surprise
was overdone

When they shot him
he flopped like a rag doll
and after he grew stiff
they dragged him to a snowbank
and stuck him upright
his eyes a glassy imitation
of blue northern skies

All winter long
his outstretched frozen arm
guided their tanks and cycles
and all the passing soldiers
laughingly said
his expression of surprise
was overdone

In Tunisia
(for Terry and Wendy Ward)

Epiphanies
did not die
altogether when
the Greeks sailed
finally, their
slack jaws
dripping
brilliance,
jars filled
with sweet
water, oars
reluctant to
part the sea
as they stared
at those lovely
Lotos-Eaters
fading westward
leaving their
indolent print
on the bright
air:
    fragments
remain—wicker
baskets spill-
ing limes whose
fragrance brings
tears; the bony
camels bearing
dark water from
wells of dried

mud; even
the Berber
in the cafe, his
djellaba flooding
the room with
light, eyes
dull with
foolishness
repeated through
centuries,
muttering his ancient
proverb (polished
like a stone
from use)
            'A
woman for
passion, a boy
for entertainment
but a goat
for sheer pleasure.'

Epiphanies
like angels
are of different orders.

Cornwall

Hungrily the salt air
pours off the flat lead plate
gnaws at the stones

of this old land, death-pocked
pitted with shrunken veins
sucked hollow, collapsed

beneath a dull green jug
crazed, bruising
the thyme where it lies

fluting its lip
in dry remembrance
of a gush & water's bright scatter

An Old Story

For an unknown reason just now
I remembered an old story with no
moral I can see.
On a lovely
summer day all liquid blue and gold
with the pigeons pink-
eyed in astonishment, a peasant
instructed a boy
in how to spear fish (fat glittering
salmon) with a nail stuck
into the wooden
handle of a scythe
but forgot as he told the boy to strike
at the fish
the bright blade of the scythe
was hanging behind and above the boy's shoulders
when he
struck (hard)
his head and one ear of his teacher
tumbled down the bank
landing
before a miller carrying sacks of flour
Whose head
is that the miller asked
I dunno answered an old man standing
next to him
and looking at what lay at
their feet
but whoever it is
he's got three ears

De Nada

beneath the white map
or chaos
of the stars
the moon floats

he stands barefoot
on the cracked
cooling earth
Nightbirds shriek

swoop
his mineral fear
makes luminous
his sweat

he waits to kill
a tank
with an old gun
that his father

killed rabbits with
and a broken-
bladed knife
but no tank appears

so at dawn he turns
to go and two
soldiers
shoot him twice

walk away
not talking
buttoning
their pistol holsters

but when the sun
makes salt
from his sweat
and he lies dying

in the flat field
nursing his
torn stomach
he tries to say

Beep-Beep

south of Denver
    on U. S. 40
    he scrabbled in the dirt
    with a knife

looking for maybe
    a bit of shard
    a fossilized mosquito
    the origins of a perfect poem

drank coffee & tinned milk
    from a metal cup
    (tasting dusty)
    ate dry biscuits

couldn't find any berries
    was constipated
    obsessed, said
    the University

a nut case
    was the way
    the locals put it
    but at last

he found a pre-speech flint
    cold as ice in the warm earth
    smelling of cactus-
    flowers

didn't notice
    what hid from him
    & his last useless act
    was to sprinkle

vinegar
    from an aluminium canteen
    on his sweaty face
    before

the jaws gleamed &
    he'd had it

Kif Poem

'Pourtant, j'étais fort mauvais poète.
Je ne savais pas aller jusqu'au bout.'

Blaise Cendrars.

I

Three weeks!
the return from exile!

under the early sun
whitewashed cubes shine on the hills
shops full of polished brass
blaze like a thousand furnaces

the exile returns!

wave to the porters
wave to the medina

I even wave at the police
who stare at me
in their grey suits and green glasses

I'm back
the swollen bureaucracies
can't touch me!

a waiter washes soap
from the windows of a cafe
they wink at me
the smiling windows of the cafe

an incense bearer nods
scatters sweet purple smoke at my feet

the sun sweeps the shadows under the buildings

a child drags a block of ice up the hill

I'm back!
Zones of sun
rinse the fog from my brain
oranges wash the crust from my teeth

I wave at the Casablanca train
chuffing from the toy station

heaps of shining black & green olives
piles of saffron
glittering swordfish, tangled squid

the exile thumbs his nose at the world!

2

Simplicities—
the walk to the cafe

hot coffee, bread
and a newspaper

the bowl of sliced oranges
sprinkled with sugar

and a cigarette
of black tobacco

3

They have given me a room
on top of a house in the medina
from the balcony I see the harbour

a white boat bounces on the blue bay

the house is whitewashed
poinsettias pour colour from the walls

the muezzin draws arabesques of sound
through mazes of telephone wires
and television antennae

I hang my feet over the balcony
and smoke kif
and feel the salt dry on my back

4
Eyes are blank here
dark with the beauty of nothingness

globes, reflecting
an earthenware jar filled with water

or a goat in a tree

their smiles
break
startling

snow-flowers
on the Anti-Atlas

5

the old Jew has a white beard
& sad, deep eyes

he sits in the sun
for his arthritis
out of the wind

his wooden chair squeaks against the plaster wall

& he opens his sad eyes
to watch four men pull iron cables
from an ox-cart

6
Christ
my trouble is
reading newspapers

drinking coffee
at a little iron table
past which walk beautiful girls

& flower vendors
& a water carrier
tinkling his brass plate

while I read
the stupidest news
with the aid of a bad dictionary

under sunlight
so strong
it hurts my eyes

the dictionary
consoles me
it tells me I am not just an object

past which walk beautiful girls

7

Beggars are respected here
they've been touched by God
if you can give them a few pennies
that's good

or just touch your forehead
as you pass
if you don't have anything

one came up to me tonight
and I had nothing
so he stood there waiting
until three policemen
took hold of him

two held him
while the third
hit him in the mouth
until he spat teeth & blood
and fell down

so they kicked him
until he stopped moving

please
if you are bothered again let us know
here we respect the tourists

8

in the cafe
everyone plays parcheesi
& watches the dancing boy

the television sulks in the corner

he dances
bird-like
in a saffron robe

the circle of musicians are stunned with kif

the boy sings
his death-zoned eyes
the sharp arabesque of mint & toilets

a pool of dazzling colour

at the feet
of the American Negress
her scarf has fallen

9

the fumes cling
with a rough cloth
and a bar of yellow soap

I wash my face
until the skin stings

my mask hides another mask

at least I have plenty of company!

10
a storm shatters the valley
frightened the trees bend away

great plants of light
sprout crazily from the ground

the air sags
under the smell of rain & ozone

on the iron roof
the rain sounds hollow

we listen
around the smoking lamp

to a report in Arabic
then in English

to a huge night raid
on the other side of the earth

flames drowning a whole city
crops under a burst dam

everyone looks at the floor

outside a dog barks & barks & barks

(*Envoi*)

a world
of busted shoes
filled with melting snow

jugs of water
from every ocean
on his work-desk

portrait
a boiled egg

a man whose face has vanished

egg dreaming of Yucatan
jungles
steaming & green

a world of sea changes

a woodcutter
with a filling station
deep in the Brazilian forest

who carves tiny wood saints
each in his meticulous
automobile

heat fresh as a bright lemon

his dream the transsiberian wind
rolling across the still-drugged wastes of Russia

& from the mouth

an old war wound

flowers

luxurious, spilling
onto just a few

of the old battlefields

F. W. Willetts

CUNARD IN THE DESERT

TO BARBARA BRAY

PART ONE

I

grain upon grain for the long drifting

so let it be

merely to be

what

and for whom

being dead

I close my eyes and still the sun stands in the heavens a wild beast ravening and distraught spreading its frustration and despair through the desert and thus resume

and thus create in order to destroy

II

so then the old quarter the estuary the gulls the boats the cold the grey the light

the old quarter

morning white radiance dazzling down on mean streets the heavens corrupted

a mid morning a Salvation Army band playing in a derelict square the women in their black stamping to the music as they sing and bang their tambourines

and on the corner stood the broken toothed vendor his steel framed mouth permanently open

and thus resume

roads on a landscape like flattened veins scattered with ashes also

shadow and sunlight in an empty yard its brick floor
warm in the sun with a few weeds groping among wet
stones in a damp corner where a pipe from a lavatory
would drip forever its stars of rust that stained
the stones

and that was eternity before the world began

to destroy

III

stale weary wastes of nightland

dry horror in the desert

a seraphic face of impeccable silence

death is instantaneous without past or future

past or future

in the streets would be children running shouting
laughing crying angry impotent gay unthinking
running this way and that the walls giving back
their echoes

and on foggy days the ships in the estuary nursed
the waters while now and then the slow flight of a
gull turned above them in the silence

drifting no longer fearing without emotion lost
with nothing to lose death is instantaneous
instantaneous instantaneous

say it till there's nothing turning above them in
the silence days and darknesses without number

IV

a supplication

for what purpose and to whom

even the sunlight is like a wound an insult to the
suffering

and resume

yesterday or the day before or this morning a car
stopped in the street beyond the wall and two men
were laughing and a woman's startled voice began
to rail and curse them then all was silent until
the car drove away then all was silent silent
silent

and resume

that summer the streets had the smell of dry plaster
but in the rain they smelt of fire

and resume

even silence has its sound

and resume

V

the dead tree by the wall is weighed down by its shadow

its silence is pitiless in a merciful world pitiless

VI

death is instantaneous instantaneous instantaneous

without past or future

in the desert only the dead have reality

only the dead must suffer the eternal damnation of the moment

and love the flame

VII

this point of despair where the mind in its anguish
moves forward into a region of ice and perpetual
night where there is no one to talk to and nothing
to say no one to love nothing to take and nothing
to give and no despair only the silence the
emptiness and the cold stare and the dumb mouth in
a cold mind and every way one turns the universe
like a sucked egg

and thus resume and thus resume and thus resume

the cobbled alley that ran down to the siding where
old Joan humped her sack of coal on Fridays gritted
her pipe between her teeth and struggled sideways
up the short slope her cracked boots gaping and
shutting as she went

VIII

above the stairs in the half light of the hall the
chandelier tinkled

a myriad tiny specks of coloured light shone on
the walls flashing a moment of wet living colour
across the stale years of brown paint

and in the morning they would hesitate as they met
in the dark of the landing and he would place his
hand against her breast or on her thigh

and she would lie in their bed listening and come
down to breakfast with the lifeless smile of
countless mornings set around her dry mouth and the
conversation would wander while her sister from
across the table envied her

and having resumed

and resume and resume and resume

IX

to be free and love the flame and not be free and
not be free

and thus resume

feeding the desert with their voices

and thus resume

and then I witnessed the long savage tumult of the
streets hour after hour as the houses were fired
and the lorries took them away and in the evening
walls cracked and fell and showers of sparks swept
up into the night sky and here and there people
crept from street to street seeking for scraps of
information scraps of hope while above them as they

went the moonlight spread its benediction through
the dark and in that beginning I lived in a space
under a roof for countless close and airless days
living from a store of tins and I remember how the
sparrows alarmed me by their fright when they saw
me fearing they would attract attention and draw
them upon me and one day there was a woman in the
room below me and after they had finished they
methodically beat her to death

and thus resume and thus resume

the knot of curious tightening on the corner by the
sea wall on a hot Bank holiday afternoon avid for
details to wrap up and carry home of how the child
fell from the pavement as the car pulled in and
the driver sat slumped over the steering wheel
champing his mouth and bringing forth from his
throat nothing but a choking sound a little tiny
sound like mice in a wainscot and the child's head
lolled loosely this way and that while the child's
father stood looking on speechless unbelieving
frozen to the pavement his mouth fallen open and
then he dropped like a stone suddenly and without
warning so that they had to drag him dirtying his
trousers to the sea wall in the shadow loosening
his collar until the ambulance came with all the

cars pulled in and took the child's poor body away
and the man came round and went away with them to
the hospital all the blood drained from his face but as
meek as meek as if nothing had happened

resume

their voices

X

drifting like a gull for scraps while the sunlight
and the silence unpicks my flesh

dry ungovernable light

and Rita when she was young

became

that old woman in her room shrieking in her
dissolution

this has no anguish save the anguish of silence of
darkness of light of shadow

of minute unwilled activities

this has no anguish shrieking in dissolution

and thus resume

the old quarter kicking itself to bits convulsion
after convulsion and then the long drawn dying
quiver of its flesh to stillness and the minute
unwilled activities of the dead

no ceremonial endless days of low mists on the river
haunted by the gulls that turn away and wail

the bare streets streets in a desert of poisonous
silence and the dead unburied ageless hours of
waiting and for what

a privet hedge blackened by the fire with one
bright soft new leaf trembling in the stillness

and this stone once rough worn smooth and that tree
frail outcrop of brittle bones casting its crooked
shadow at my feet

if I count all the bricks I can see I shall not have begun

XI

shall not have begun

as boys running in a flail of light across the
marshes to the old boat standing with its riven
planks in the river the smell of fish and sea-
weed and the man who died there crawling from the
water to freeze in the darkness a place to terrify
and enchant a place to smoke pilfered cigarettes
and hunt in packs and die and die again and
remember now remember now in this place where the
rats go hungry and the wind no longer brings its
ancient tidings Saturday jostlings and men haunted
by soft forgiving flesh in the longed for dark and
Sundays and rain falling on listless afternoons
monotony sprawling in every chair turning again to
the brief past and feeling only rancour after
satisfaction and seeking satisfaction out of
rancour and dull and unresisting known and certain
learn and never learn the lost ways before the ways
were known never return only to know that unknowing
that satisfaction could never be known or known
known once and once only fleetingly as the moment
passed from unknowing to unknowing dwindling into
unreality the dull routine of evil dwindling until
all that we possess is the sense of what is lost

and being lost and losing perpetually losing losing
and not holding no longer holding no longer caring
no longer even not caring until at last between
these walls only the wind frets and yet even now I
hear her voice walking in the sunlight and cling to
it listening and wonder what it was she felt all
that pain all that distress so long ago and afterwards to know that overwhelming surfeit of love
turn to wretchedness and wretchedness to mute
desolation in a mind raving in the silence and the
house was dumb unreal remote the same and not the
same and all things in it were touched with the
same dumbness and the garden was suddenly crushed
by the sky and the trees and grass died and went
on living and that was how it was I had died and
went on living her death her death was when the
world died

XII

questing and questless dry light falling on days
long dead undaunted in their progress

and that time that time insisting always

a swing in a garden that made the apples swim in
blueness

making it possible bearable unbearable impossible

XIII

I crawled one night into this place and turning saw
the gap behind me built over brick by mounting
brick until the task was done and the ringing of
the trowel had ceased and when I shouted I received
no answer

XIV

grain upon grain for the long drifting

so let it be

merely to be a witness of the tumult of scattered
light falling in the silence

and thus pour forth your benediction on my soul

XV

and resume

and resume

and resume

and resume

and

resume

PART TWO

I

slow welling pressure of despair

even in the

say it till there's nothing turning above them in
the silence days and

enough for pity

II

so then

and

III

grain on   enough for   pity   this rasp of iron
   merely to be   I close my eyes   and thus create
   their thin   their thin   tormented smiles   the
greasy nights   unable to help

the quality of witnesses is such   such that they
must exist   always   create always

the hot cruel town   sweltering under   thunder
   mauve and smoking twilight   crushed to a whisper
   through the desert   grey light   and old   was a
beginning   roads in a landscape   flattened veins
   scattered with ashes

ashes

wastes of   nightland   drifting   no longer

laughing as I took her   the summer streets
   ceasing to laugh   the waning twilight   crushed
to a whisper   the town

crushed to a whisper

IV

the half light

the half light   their voices   envied her   their voices   the half light   their   voices   cloying quick furtive amorous resentful bored lonely dull complacent safe

not safe not safe her death

merely to have been   not enough   a witness   and thus to have made it endless

of the tumult   the tumult   meek as   of the tumult
how could they   not speechless   understand   how it felt   understand   it felt   not speechless the mind   raving   ravening   raving   not   believing not believing   not   accepting

drifting waiting shrieking in her dissolution
drifting waiting shrieking

low mists on the river the houses collapsing
the trees standing in water collapsing the
stumps of trees the wind from the marshes
sweeping its salt flail of bitter light his
battered face washed too long puckered white
pitted green scum the gulls the gulls above
the quiet

monotony of Sunday

V

mute love mind raving questless lightless falling wordless no longer answering no longer answering

grain on

light fall

VI

broken voices   cold corridors   chattering and
white coated   no longer there   mindless   seeing
them smiling   mindless   trying to comprehend
their glances   then again   the lone corridors
   hour in   not mindless   anguished

in the hallway   clutching   clinging   on the
pavement a crowd   gathered   curious   and pitying

drowning in the twilight   the upturned white face
   fingers groping   for my hand   and my hand on the
rail   of the stairs   unable to reach her   for the
crowd   unable to reach her   unable to reach her
   unable to save her   from the drowning   the
twilight   the faces peering   down   lost in
shadows

groping

VII

in the market   everything suddenly   incredibly
old   shabby and   ailing

old crones round the   fountain dry   as plaster
  and the throngs   rustling like leaves   stiff
dead leaves   screeching   when they touched   the
sunlight on them   like a furnace   and their
thoughts   roosting in the windows   black and
ravening   when they smiled   invisible claws drew
  down their faces   lines of anguish

their raw mouths and eyes bled   but unheeded

VIII

unheeded unheeded for the long and still the
sun going on forever reverberating forever
  morning white radiance on a low wall drinking
  from a child's mug the liquid lilting across
her face ribbons of sunlight far off

far off far off

weary wastes dry horror no longer running
  shouting

running

running shouting laughing crying angry impotent gay
unthinking

ships in the estuary   nursed the waters

all that is left   hardly to   death   without
number   white a white   forever

in the water   the ripples widen   crazy timbers
   green and   steaming   churn back the low   wet
swish of dull   returning waters   easing from the
estuary   the refuse of the dying

the old quarter   the old quarter

frozen

no way out   no way in   no way back   no way
forward

champing his mouth bringing forth minute
unwilled activities no longer shrieking in
  dissolution and then the long drawn dying
  quiver of the flesh and the minute unwilled
  activities of the dead all that is left far
back far back merely to have been a witness
  and thus and thus to have made it

endless

IX

unravelled   and unravelling silence

haaaaaaaaaaaaaaaaaaaaaaaaaaaaaaaaaaaaaaaaaaaaaaaaaaaaaaaa
h

X

crushed to a whisper   to live forever   being
dead   wastes of nightland   of the desert   no
longer   waiting for the   bush to burn   the
summer streets to burn   and after   the nights
  scattered with ashes   running with ghosts   the
low clouds   giving back   their dull clamour
  waiting for thunder   the ships on fire   in the
estuary   turned the sunlight yellow   all that
  all that   was nothing   crushed to a whisper
  the streets   the tumult   ravening   the houses
  the silence   collapsing   the streets   too hot
to walk in   the wind from the marshes   sweeping
its flail   of bitter light   and afterwards   and
afterwards   the

gulls calling

above the quiet

XI

the quiet   to a whisper   being dead   past
emotion   was nothing   the sunlight   turned to
yellow   among the shadows   stooping out of   the
heavens   a whisper

a low clamour   and the dog   barking in the yard
  hysterical   yapping   in the lightning
  cowering   in its corner   shivering   whining
  its shadow   in the lightning   thrown shrunken
  and   black against   the wall   and   the houses
  of the street were   silent   silent   and black
  mindless   but in

but in   this house   all   was activity   the
clock past midnight   and then the small hours
  and still the child   torn   from its sleeping
  its uneasy torpor   its weakening   still
clutching   twisting   weak and unavailing
  against   pain   that racked every nerve   until
screaming   was not   not enough   to satisfy the
God   of anguish   was not enough   not   enough
  never enough   to satisfy   the dull routine   of

evil   the house was dumb   unreal remote   the
same   and not

the house was dumb   unreal remote   the same   and
not

was not enough

the same

the house was dumb unreal remote the same and not the same and all things in it were touched with the same dumbness

and the garden and the garden crushed to a whisper

and the garden

crushed by the sky   that room above the garden
  listening to the birds   far back   another time
  far back   another time   another world
  scattered with ashes   merely to be   with nothing
  achieved   except the dead   unhurried days
  surveillance   a nightmare   by the dead   living
with the dead   the waning   the waning twilight
  seeking for a way   across the marshes   and the
gulls   and the gulls   wheeling   haunting   a few
crippled trees   mostly willows   burned out hulks
  and thin   smears   of oil   colouring the brown
sloth   of the river   their voices   of the river
  in the half light   following their voices   that
voice   all afternoon   seeking   fearing drowning
  fearing a   down turned face lying in the shallows
  and to come   to this   far back   far back   to
this   that end   this end   and to come upon them
  in the hollow   among rotting palings   merry as
crickets   mindless   unthinking   of our grievings
  and no   they had not heard   our calling   our
voices   in the marshes   for they had been playing
all afternoon   among the palings   and safe   and
safe   playing   and anger   and love   were
  uppermost   the walk home   the twilight   waning
  the path damped by the evening   the low mist
  rising from the river   the hulks   in hiding   an
old pump   labouring   vomiting forth black water
from a ditch   that suddenly filled   you with fear

fear the dead man   in the river   when they turned
  his face   his mouth swilled out   black water

filled with fear

enough   what was it   enough   what was it   enough
  the wheeling   picked bare   the smears of oil
  spreading   through the waters   unwound and
  unwinding   among the shadows   unwound and
  unwinding   enough for pity

grain on grain

mauve and smoking twilight   crushed to a whisper
  through the desert   grey light   dry horror
  in the desert   was a beginning   in a landscape
  drifting   scattered with ashes   drifting   death
masks   in the market   on the stalls   summer
  summer streets   crushed to a whisper   not
speechless   not accepting   not accepting   such
dissolution   between the   drifting   the shadows

the scattered light   made a witness   how it felt
forever   light fall   on broken voices   clutching
in the hallway   clinging   drowning   in the
twilight   the upturned face   drowning   the
waning   half light   of the marshes   black water
falling   through their peering   unable   unable to
save her   from their voices   unable to
unavailing   lost in shadows   unable to help her
in the market   incredibly   old   wizened in
anguish   and old   old   and the throngs   old
rustling like leaves   the sunlight   on them
like a furnace   screeching   screeching   when
they smiled   invisible claws drew   down their
faces   bleeding and   unheeded   and still   and
still the   sun above the garden   fell through the
blossoms   of that Easter   on a low wall   drinking
from her child's mug   mindless   of the tumult
breaking around her   of love   of love   of love
emptying   forever about her   to keep her safe
safe   not safe   not safe   her death   weary
wastes of nightland   in the desert   among the
throngs   screeching in the market   in the desert
without number   no   no   no   far back   far
back   before that time   that time   and   and
green was green   and blue   blue was blue   and
all things   all things   all things   all that
time   is left   hardly to know   death is   so
complete   she said   without number   nursed the
waters   out of the blackness   all that is   left
in the desert   in the ripples   the crazy timbers
green   and   churn back   white a white   the
refuse of the dying   the blossoms   held   the
sunlight   the white sunlight   once   and once

only drowning and dangerous dangerous such
whiteness at Easter dying the old quarter
sent to the fire without blessing such
whiteness lost forever never enough the
dissolution never enough the shrieking hour
after hour hour after hour the shrieking to
be dead merely to have been a witness such pity
and worthless no no no no such no
such whiteness lost and thus to have made it
endless not crushed to a whisper merely no
but terrible sonorous anguish filling the mind
and endless not merely but left enough just
enough to pity to pain to die and die again
there here there forever nights of dumb
disaster running with ghosts the low clouds
give back their clamour waiting for thunder
the houses collapsing the streets too hot to
walk in and the wind from the marshes came
like a shield of fire and for days the fires
raged the town reeled and fell and for always
in dry summers whenever it rained the streets
smelt of fire of ancient anguish lies of
people running clutching clinging with with
nothing to cling to to save them in the desert
in the anguish of the desert to have been a
witness until screaming was not enough and all
formal rites had been observed the doors
opened and shut leaving the anti-chamber bereft
of purpose and they all filed out into the
rain the cold feeling it was not enough
never enough and the day was not the same
unreal remote the same and not the same how
could it ever living with the dead the waning

scattered with ashes   a nightmare   a desert
the waning   all their   faces   of the desert
so to that final Sunday   the gulls above the
marshes   wheeling   in the quiet   derisive   and
scorning   angry with my coming   following their
voices   and his voice   his voice   among them
silent   drowned   calling   when   they called
his face   his mouth swilling out   black water
and the gulls   the gulls mocking laughter
unwinding in the sunlight   a darkness   a
darkness   that was   unending

neverhowelsecoulditbenever   enough   enough for
pity   inthedesert   inthedeserthowitfeltnever
enough   and the garden   sunlit blossoms of that
Easter   to cling   never   neverenoughtoclingto
saytopitytodieneverenoughtoappease   no   no longer
drifting   on that Sunday   finished   with the
quiet of the marshes   the heavens   finished with
the   crushed to a whisper   a whispercrushedtoa
whisperinthequietneverrelinquishedhowitfelthowcould
iteverbedumborfinishednotfinisheddisasterinthestreets
neverhowcoulditevernoneverthesamethequietthedying
waningtwilightskiesabovethemarshesfinishedhidingmy
dyingmyunendingwaningdarknesslikemyunendingdarkness
likemyunendingdarknessnolongerthesamenolongerenough
thescreamingthegullsscreamingoutoftheirvoicesenough
sorrowingthedeadunderthedeadskieswaningabovethedying
marsheshowcoulditeverhavematteredgoneonmatteredand
goneonexceptinthatthisthereheredyingupturnedface
clingingaskingforloveunabletoloveloveloveunableto
loveunabletoanymorethesameandnotthesamethesameending
unendingunwoundunwoundandunwindinginthedarkoftheday

thesunthesuninthedarkofthedaydaydesertthroughtheday
thedesertthetownthedesertdrowningandthelappingwaters
swelledandbrokeinsidehisheadtheclamourofthedyingthe
dyinglivingofthelowheavensupbraidingslightsoslighta
mockingturnedtolaughterfeedingthedesertwiththat
laughterlaughterfortheunendingdesertinthedesertin
thetwilightafterthewaningthedissolutionthescreaming
thewaningthelongunendingendoftheirvoicescallingfar
backfarbackalltogetherbrokenontheirvoicestheir
voiceslostwavessplinteringandupbraidingturnedto
laughtersuchlaughtersuchmockerysuchanguishmockery
laughterneverenoughnoneveranguishofanguishturnedto
anguishturnedtoalowwhispercrawlinglikeawormthrough
theslimethegutstheanguishofthepastunendingbegun
merelyunendingfeedingthedesertfeedingonwormsworms
makingthedeserthabitablefortheunendingentrailsofthe
pastlockedtailtomouthtocreateoftheunendingnomatter
ofwhathowelsewhatelseforloveforloveforloveforlove
forlovecrawledheretailtomouththroughblackwatersthe
skiesvomitinglightforthescatteredthelostthelonethe
anguishedforsuccourneverlightonthelostnolonger
havingnothinghavinghavingdyingtailtomouthcreating
outoftheblackwatersthesIimethevomitthelightlight
lightneverscatteredlightandawhiteawhitevoices
crushedmuteraveningravingunendingsuchhungerneverto
losenevertosuchraveningappeasedneverunappeased
sonorousclamourinthequietturnedtoanguishanguish
underthelowheavensandthelightundiminishedthelies
farbackdriftingfarbacknotenoughtohidetolosetodie
underthelowheavenscrawlingtowardsthelostthelost
remaderemadetailtomouthremadenevertoknowhowmuch
nevertoknowhowmuchlovewhatitwashowsuchneverenoughto
giveandgiveandgiveandtoendlikethisgladlynoneverto
knowunavengedcrawlingthroughwhatthepasttheanguish
thelightfallingtheeyespeeringhereevenherecalling
thevoicesatlasttowardsfeelingawaytowardsthelow
heavensmeetingtowardsdumbunendingtolovetosaveonlyto
easesuchdissolutiontoeasetoeaseneverlonelostfailing
driftingalonedriftingalonedriftingtoeasetoeasenot

enoughnotenoughonlythedesert

haaaaaaaaaaaaaaaaaaaaaaaaaaaaaaaaaaaa
h
haaaaaaaaaaaaaaaaaaaaaaaaaaaaaaaaaaaaaaaaaaaaaaaaa
h
haaaaaaaaaaaaaaaaaaaaaaaaaaaaaaaaaaaaaaaaaaaaaaaaaaaaaaaaaaaaa

PART THREE

I

is enough only the desert alone lost is
enough dyinglivingofthelowheavensupbraiding
light never for the unending locked tail to
mouth tailtomouthtocreateoutoftheunendingnomatter
whatofwhatofhowofitofdyinglivingwaningreachingnever
obtainingtheraveningragesreturninglosingwhatelse
thereisnonenoonethetwilightravinggoneandravinglight
fallingnooneonlyofthepastvomitingmalevolencepeering
regardingeyeredsavageinthedarklowheavensraging
unsatisfiedwithwhatofwhatof

	unsatisfied		
	unsatisfied		
	remorseless		
	darkness		
	and		
	light		
	there		
derisive	peering		
dead	seeking		
leering	in		
unable	or		
to	out		
return	never	how	
derisive	ending	else	
darkness	since	there	
that	only	unending	
savage	to	there	
red	retain	questing	
eye	hold	broken	such
peering	have	broken	sorrow
unknowing	unbroken	how	such
peering	the	else	patient
of	days	their	suffering
what	those	laughter	unending

blossoms	of	never	their	and
of	whom	returning	unending	never
that	peering	days	smiles	to
sunlight	to	of	betraying	know
out	understand	days	and	how
of	malevolent	of	betrayed	much
air	in	joy	betrayed	love
out	the	and	they	was
of	silent	sorrow	lived	there
anguish	malevolent	and	being	to
anguish	eye	blessed	dead	shed

out	understand	days	and	how
of	malevolent	of	betrayed	much
air	in	joy	betrayed	love
out	the	and	they	was
of	silence	sorrow	lived	there
anguish	malevolent	and	being	to
anguish	eye	blessed	dead	shed

of				
air				
of				
anguish				
	the			
	silence			
		and		
		blessed		
			being	
			dead	
				much
				love

of the and being much
anguish silence blessed dead love

of the and being much
anguish silence blessed dead love

red
savage
unheeded
bleeding
convulsed
and
broken
and
blessed
in
the
night
unable
to
anymore
blessed
felt
it
the
last
bitter
ravening
rearing
blessed
broken
and
bleeding

and
bleeding
unheeded

unable
to
turn

calling

II

the
house
was
full
of
that
morning
quiet

that
morning
quiet
before
the
fires
were
lit

and
everything
was
fresh

unconscious
and
unseen

before
the
day

in
the
garden
the
sunlight
fell
like
a
brush
stroke

like
a
brush
stroke
through
the
leaves

and
the
trees

listening
to
this

their
voices
out
of

this
voice
broken
and

diminished
out
of
this
voice
crawling

crawling
away

on
the
wind

the
sounds
of

insects

in
the
house

in
the
house
there
was
no
help
anymore
no
help
anymore

everywhere
in
the
garden

the
scent
of
new
leaves

new
leaves

everywhere

the
air
was
full
of
it

new
leaves
full
of

and

begins		to		the
the		die	how	day
brutalities		rootless	could	
the		restless	there	became
exhaustion		anywhere	be	uneasy
the	stood	alone	to	conscious
futilities	mantled	only	witness	and
the	in	and	such	uneasy
exhaustion	their	yet	losing	flinching
the	private	only	hour	from
repetitive	mysteries	only	by	the
petty		to		days
annihilations		go		brutalities
of	and	on		
what	the	whispering		
it	hedges	a	nothing	
could	breathed	new	availing	
be		life		
	and	out		conscious
what	stirred	of		and
it		the		uneasy
could	and	old		
	stirred			
				of
what	their	out		something
it	private	of	nothing	old
could	mysteries	the	availing	forgotten
what	their	brutalities	availing	something
it	private	brutalities	nothing	old
could	mysteries	brutalities	availing	forgotten

what
it
could

old

old

old old

III

repetitive
minute
annihilations

of
what
it
was
once

to be in the desert not
in the desert half in the desert aware and
unaware of the desert oneself the desert
repetitive minute annihilations nothing else
availing

nothing
else
availing

the
desert
this
night
of
despair unending this
night of losing of having lost from the
beginning

lost
from
the
beginning

always   always   always   always

IV

minute	minute	these	listening	too
unwilled		crusts	for	far
activities		of	a	back
	crusts		difference	
	of			too
to	indifference		in	far
go		these	the	off
on		crusts		
	minute	of		
	crusts	love	silence	too
to	of			far
go				back
on			a	
	how		difference	
	it		of	
and		turned		too
complete	will	stale	the	far
	be			off
being			silence	
incomplete				
				now
always				
				to
always				be
				certain

that
pain
was

waiting
for
the
slow

VI

for
ever
and
ever

from
the
depths
of

without
end
to
it

such
twisting

of
the
knife

to
watch
and
say

say

standing
waiting
smiling

for
the
eyes

to
open

open
these
eyes

those
eyes

for
the
eyes
to
open

never
now
anymore
for
these
eyes

needless

worthless
to
resist
the

flood
the
avalanche

to
be
buried

buried
and
done
with

best
thing
best
thing

she
said
done
with

world
without

void
and
null

the
centre
of

of
how
say
it

fix
it

how
reach
out

touch

hold

have

bright
this

what

circle
of

never
resisting
like
a
fairground
this

lighted
vistas
richly
coloured

worthless
light

this
bright
bracelet
of
despair

nailed
across

made
to
laugh

made
to

made
to

lying
in
the
half
light

wandering

in
death

the
death
the
streets
quiet
after
rain

no
longer
living
in
the
world

walked

why
that
was
how
it
was

startled

as
if
this
were
the
utter
end
of
folly

the
dawn
of

who
can
say

a
dawn

a
dawn

no
more

my
friend
if
only
you
knew

out
of
the
dumb
silence
will
come

their
wills
ride

their
smiling
wills

ride
the
little
waves

ah
if
only

my
friend

a
matter
of

in
the
dusk

the
streets
were
quiet
after
rain

begin
again
begin
again

the
quiet

ah
my
friend

if
only
you
knew

this
is
no
end

no
end

we
can't
live

we
live

we
can
not
live
forever
in
the
past

ah
my
friend

I
hold
so
dear

I
feel
so
close

I
understand

I
understand

believe
me

all
night
the
skies
weighed
down

such
need

only
a
matter
of

need
I
say

at
all

but
walking
in
knowledge

knowledge

such
feelings
what
words

what

words

VIII

voices	how	like	clean	never
in	shall	a	slate	give
this	it	dream	clean	in
dark	be	it	break	never
strange	possible	will	that	say
unravelling	not	be	is	die
dissecting	possible	like	the	not
lost	bearable	a	only	what
never	never	bad	way	intended

no	yes	dream	to	wished
longer	of	of	go	for
cling	course	something	forward	the
and	lies	forgotten	untainted	memory
unremember	live	of	learn	the
unravel	by	the	out	memory
for	lies	past	of	will
the	no	past	sorrow	lose
lost	never	recall	to	its

the	yes	how	live	terror
light	always	it	to	its
dwindling	never	was	live	anguish

the	never	it	to	its

hush	surely	will	live	sorrow
the	such	seem	never	its
light	way	distant	enough	yes
the	such	far	remember	yes
laughter	knowing	off	yes	yes
in	wake	not	remember	that
the	one	real	but	is
streets	morning	a	the	how
their	and	dream	good	it
streets	wake	not	not	must
vaunted	no	real	only	be
vaunted	it	it	the	to
always	cannot	will	bad	understand
never	be	be	side	understand
the	like	strange	of	inspite
same	that	at	things	of
again	will	first	the	this
this	not	strange	bad	inspite
night	yes	to	moments	of
of	yes	feel	so	the
the	yes	so	many	lost
desert	yes	different	yes	lost
the	one	so	so	on
black	day	free	many	never
unfathomable	a	as	but	it
ways	new	if	not	can
of	beginning	all	always	never
longing	like	were	here	be
pity	like	new	is	lost

what pity what suffering not enough to

out of

old forgotten forgiven forgive yourself

alive forgotten forgiven must forgive

sense real sense the yes the bad was

but will remain must remain no never it

atone for living for going on living
the dumb silence will not end at all no
no never the atonement the atonement
voices this strange dark this
and let live what is left to live let
speaking it a dream
bad but the good was real more real how
in the
is gone dead done with no no no no

not living and not living living yes

more finish that no more how else on

the atonement not enough yes yes will

all without pity turning away turning

live and live to the full what else is

a blessing in could not say enough

it really was the bad will fade what

in rain that time and the laughter

no irreversibly never again never again

living saying good morning smiling
the wind the something on the wind
be must be or die die living have
embarrassed saying must go wanting
there must turn away from all that
convulsed and broken convulsed not easy
it was was love love in the street
tears of all that no more how say all
that laugh that voice it must be

talking nodding walking never enough
no no the hollow dead mouths talking
died no never but go on only repetitive
to seem so right proper on the stairs
so far back once more rather than lose
mercy to share nothing only to want
he sun shining on the trees still wet
that no more not enough must suffer
even in the silence peering up asking

only yes it would again without
telling and retelling private
minute annihilations
the stairs but it was past
no will lose lose all
the pain to end the thread of
from the rain all new and
what no never the same
for help there was none

IX

from the marshes from the beginning
among their private mysteries they
gulls calling one bright merely
in the house there was no help
time when the days were dumb dumb
how else their laughter their
these crusts of love nothing else
morning white radiance before the
conscious and uneasy flinching

ravening undaunted
and thus take stock
celebrate the unliving
how shall we
to have once to have had
once
anymore no how else how
never
to say when the skies
broken
unending smiles betraying
go back
availing and even love
no longer now
sorrows before the world
of the tumult the
from the days unending

X

```
h t d o a t o h t h c t f t t a n
e o a u l h n o h e o h o h h n o
a   y t l e c w o r u e r u a d
r r s       e   s   g     s t   l
  i   o g d   e e f h e e   s s o
t n s f o e c l   a i y v i   m n
h g u   n s o s y c n e e t f i g
e   c t e e u e e e g s r   a l e
i t h h   r l   a         w i i r
r h   e h t d h r l o t a a r n
  e b   o     o s i u o n s   g l
b   r b   l s w   k t   d   t   i
r h i l n i p   l e   o   o h w v
o e g a e g e e o   b p e n a h i
k a h c v h a v s l l e v c t e n
e r t k e t k e t o o n e e s n g
n t     r     r   v o   r
                  e d
```

nuocabaygl i abi tultf ti swt cntsar
onnrnl nei i t nenhnehohni ahro hone
t r t udads vgcdyt eqter et pke ymi s s a
bahst ccoi has ohi ut ss chpi di oswwr
eve hukannt noneri ht uoei nanr l eei
l ewer dl egdnt ddve er cr pngygeaer n
i l i dnal dbr ehpeot dehr agas t t st s g
el nt eyaaayvai si dwer i r tnt huti t a
vi dods nycaet t ecai t adkedher t t hb
i nt at adaknrwyr er ns vot akegnhwee
nghwhhcnndbaots kdaer hi nr ubi ard
gseheyaeoaesr f ut l rns enool as s es
ni vi delwnnl i r r nhi ei cstwul cot ao
ol os us l bedot eoeenqnowhi tsknhr a
t ei pl baevus ammndgugl i eni t aceek
ancel l ngentl ondal i ddns gnhnegne
ccer oadi r r tl r oi yi ei l gui eedj r od
ce smf cnnaehs swns gtsi s nnas l uanw
encot kennmoaeogdhas gwos l pi s sei
poachdvi yi s i onbi t fohhnt l r vt sot
tml keaent t edr aemf tl t e t aai eot nh
i o l ewyr ght dapl ni oeuor hnl nanhl b
nr i das nai i al awenr rt f eet i ggceyl